Stay Close
Jee Booze
8-10-2014

Poems by Joe

Books One & Two Combined

"with additional poems to stimulate your mind"

Joseph Booze

authorHOUSE

AuthorHouse™
1663 Liberty Drive
Bloomington, IN 47403
www.authorhouse.com
Phone: 1-800-839-8640

© 2012 Joseph Booze. All rights reserved.

No part of this book may be reproduced, stored in a retrieval system, or transmitted by any means without the written permission of the author.

Published by AuthorHouse 10/17/2012

ISBN: 978-1-4772-5379-3 (e)
ISBN: 978-1-4772-5380-9 (sc)

Library of Congress Control Number: 2012913467

Any people depicted in stock imagery provided by Thinkstock are models, and such images are being used for illustrative purposes only.
Certain stock imagery © Thinkstock.

Because of the dynamic nature of the Internet, any web addresses or links contained in this book may have changed since publication and may no longer be valid. The views expressed in this work are solely those of the author and do not necessarily reflect the views of the publisher, and the publisher hereby disclaims any responsibility for them.

Acknowledgments

I want to thank Mrs. Kimberli Bell for her assistance, and a special thanks to my daughter Christine who lovingly helped make this project happen. Finally, I dedicate this book to my wife Veronica.

Buzz the Bee

Old Buzz left the beehive to be on his own,
but for the life of him, he couldn't
leave people alone.

He loved to buzz around your head,
buzzing some crazy song; and got the nerve
to expect you to sing along.

It's no use telling Buzz you are not a singer,
because with a smile he'll point to his stinger.

Now if you ever were stung by a bee,
you know it hurts really bad, so it wouldn't
be smart to make old Buzz mad.

Buzz isn't a bad bee, as bees go,
but he's a little pushy and needs to take it slow.

There are a lot of birds out here
that wouldn't put up with Buzz's mess
and wouldn't think twice about taking him
to their nest.

Buzz needs help; this we all know,
but who's going to tell him so?

Maybe someone can go to the beehive
and talk to the queen bee, to tell Old Buzz to let us be.

Now the Queen told us, and it ain't funny,
but Buzz been high for some time on day-old honey.

Growing Near

She does not sound the same as before;
could this be a sign that angels
are calling for her at heaven's door?

At times like this, I never know the right
thing to say, but being a friend of the angels,
maybe they will grant me a wish and keep
her due date at bay.

There is no need to tell them about her undying love
and what she means to us all. If their records
did not reflect such, they wouldn't be the ones
making the call.

Their God

Isn't it amazing that when the inevitable happens
on this earth and damage is done, some say
that it is due to man's sin; that it is something God has done.

I would like to meet their God, to see what
turns him on and gives him joy to bring
about such hurt during earthquakes, great fires,
and cyclones.

I always thought of these things as a normal
fact of life, occurring somewhere
on this earth on any given day, not someone's
God at work, making man pay.

When I see people suffering and dying
or children burned, no way are they going to
convince me that some God has done this
just to make man learn.

As a child I was told of a God that is loving
and caring and has my best interest at heart.
I think I'll stay with this one and keep the
other God apart.

Birdseed

They toss their words about like
seeds for hungry birds, to feed
those that are empty and craving
the word.

They speak with such authority,
using powerful, motivating words,
with the help of microphones;
and picture screens to ensure
they are seen and heard.

They used to talk about hell, faith,
and the heavenly gate, but now
their words are all about political
matters and those of race.

When did they stray away from
their calling, if they were ever called,
to speak about matters that they seem
to know nothing about at all?

The empty need to go elsewhere
to find the food they need; the only
thing they will get from these
speakers is more birdseed.

Christine and Lilly

My daughter and her dog are quite a pair;
who controls whom is still up in the air.
As I watch the two of them go through
their playful routine, it's the funniest
sight I have ever seen.

Get the ball Lilly. Lilly, go. What's
the problem? Why so slow? Watch me
fetch it; I'll show you what you are to do.
When I return, then it will be up to you.

As you can see, I didn't have to run very far,
or very fast. Please pay attention when
I am talking to you, and stop digging in the grass.

Now that's really impolite, turning your head and
sticking your nose in the air as if you don't care.
If you think I am fetching the ball again, you have
another thought coming. Stop smacking
your lips, you are not funny.

My Poems

My poems are like my family,
who are loving and caring, ready
to reach out, not afraid of sharing.

When I read my poems, I let the words
freely flow, allowing them to touch
a heart or two as they go.

I love to see the looks on faces,
especially when there's a smile;
I know then that the words have
awakened a good feeling deep inside.

Sometimes the smiles may be joined
by tears, but that's okay, because when
you allow words to enter your heart, it
heeds all the words that have been said.

While reading and seeing the smiles and
tears upon your face, I know that I
must hurry to write again to take others to
this joyous place.

Meet the Press

I sent my poems off with so much pride,
but after hearing what was to become
of them, I was horrified.

A bit sad because they were sent with
such high hopes, but the way they were to
be displayed struck me as a joke.

I asked that they be returned.
Many have said they are good poems
and want to take them home.

It was their first trip to a publisher, and I
was not impressed with the people they met.

They seem to have had no interest in the words,
only the money, and a rush to their press.

The Light of Day

Without the light of day, you may not see the flowers
and all the beautiful colors they display.

Without the light of day, you may hear the birds
but not see them as they gracefully fly away.

Without the light of day, you may not see a friend
smile while the two of you are at play.

Without the light of day, you may feel the snow
upon your face but not see all its wonder before
it melts away.

But one thing you will always see, even without
the light of day, is a clear path to heaven when Jesus
washes your sins away.

Excitement

What can it be; signs everywhere with the names
of McCain, Obama, and Hillary.

What a scene; laughing and joking while waiting
for their turns at the voting machine.

But something seemed to happen to them after they cast
their vote. They all reappeared as if someone had played
a very bad joke.

We may never know what changed their moods,
but there alone; maybe they realized
that this isn't a laughing matter, that things must improve.

The Waterhole

While walking in the desert with Grace and Bryce
today, Grace was doing just fine and was happily at play.
But when we came to this waterhole and Grace was told
not to walk therein; that's when all the screaming
began.

She screamed so loud for all to hear; even the birds
from miles around flew away in fear. She screamed
for her mom because Papa Joe said no, and said she'd
had enough of the desert and wanted to go.

When she returned home still screaming at the top of her
lungs, she then told her mom what Papa Joe had done.
But when her mom asked her why her shoes were all wet,
She screamed even more and said, "that's what started
all this mess."

Spoken Words

When the words of love were spoken,
you were there, then, promising
each other never to forget as they were
softly spoken again and again.

The power of those words has brought
you to this point, even replacing some
things from the past you no longer
need or want.

You've allowed these precious love words
to go deep within, sheltering them like
precious gold, making a solemn promise
to increase their value as the two of you
grow old.

Always think back to the beginning,
remembering those words—*when*
and *where*—never forgetting the
uncontrollable joy and warm love
you both felt while there.

Friendship

Love and prayers are needed without delay
the Spirit of Darkness has attacked this dear friend,
and it must be driven away.

The fight may be long and hard, but don't despair;
the Spirit of Darkness will weaken more the more you care.
Bring strong love, because this spirit does not fight
fair; it will test more than once the love you share.

You must be willing to stay in the battle as long
at it may take; this dear friend we fight for has
a lot at stake. His family is waiting one by one
for his joyful return; therefore, you must not falter
until victory is won.

The Spirit of Darkness will not leave on its own accord,
so fight hard for this dear friend with all the strength
and love you can afford.

The N Word

The N word is still used by some
allowing it to slip easily from their
tongue. Sadly they are unaware, or don't care,
that this word was sung before many
were hung.

When the N word is used, it's honoring
its creators, who couldn't be contained
as they danced and cheered while
causing so much hurt and pain.

Years have passed, and many of these
wicked men and women have long
gone to their graves to stand before
the maker, but I doubt if any will
be saved.

This one word has so many meanings,
all of which are very demeaning.
It doesn't matter how or in what
form the N word is used, you bring
disrespect to those who were and are abused.

Home

While taking a rest on the trail alone, for no apparent
reason I turned over this stone. To my surprise this
bug screamed out, *"what if I turned over your home?"*
Before I could say I didn't mean any harm,
he was already walking up my arm.

I tried to keep him in view, because this was something
I had never seen. He was wearing these big, fuzzy, red
slippers and carrying a rolled-up magazine.

He didn't say a word, just whacked me across the nose
and motioned with his magazine that I should find
another place to enjoy the forest scene. Wide eyed
and shocked, giving him no lip, I replaced the stone
that was his home very carefully with a gentle flip.

The Traveler

The roads you travel will have many turns,
but no matter which one you take, there's
a lesson to be learned. Start your journey
wisely, because all roads are not clear;
watch for danger signs, because they will appear.

Be aware of those roads that are marked
"One Way"; you may not be able to turn
in time before a toll must be paid. Use the light
you carry wisely; don't allow it to fade; you must
be able to see the potholes and the steep
hills we all dread.

Seek help from the Traveler; he will always
be near, because if your map was misprinted,
he will show you which roads are free and
those requiring a heavy fee. The roads of life
have many turns, but no matter which one you take,
there's a lesson to be learned.

Morning Cup

Why are they grinning and staring at me?
Can't they see I just want to read the
morning paper while sipping my coffee.

Even after turning a bit toward the door,
is it my imagination? Their grinning
and staring seem to be worse than
before.

Who are these people; they are strangers
to me. Why don't they stop all the grinning
and staring so I can drink my coffee?

Would you believe they are up and walking
my way. Not knowing them, what on earth
could they possibly have to say?

Well I'll be darned, they walked right by to a
lady holding a baby humming a soft lullaby.
Now I'm grinning and staring as they did before.
Is it my imagination, or did that person over there
just turn his chair towards the door?

Those Among Us

On any given day, just up the road
a way, you won't believe what you
will see. But I'm here to tell you,
it always surprises me.

I'm standing here looking at a sofa,
a stove, and a broken TV; plus old, dead
palm trees and piles of trash. I bet that
old car over there, when new, cost a lot of cash.

What sort of people would
do this to this land? Are they lacking
in pride, having no shame? I would love to
be near, should they be caught, as they
explained their twisted thoughts.

Week after week students from
Bailey Middle School gather
with their large yellow plastic bags
to do their best to clean up this
senseless mess.

It's sad we have people living among
us that show such lack of taste and
dump trash all over this place. It
wouldn't be bad if they had no other
way, but who among us hasn't
heard of trash pickup day?

Note: This was written in honor of the students at Bailey Middle School that participated in their school cleanup project on East Lake Mead Boulevard, approximately one mile east of Hollywood Boulevard

Heaven Sent

It's falling from heaven so clear and warm,
a welcome sight during this gentle storm.

We have been without rain for such a long
time, so why would anyone complain
or whine?

Let's hope enough will keep falling to water all
the flowers and trees, plus much more to
fill other dry needs.

Look up to heaven, let it fall softly upon
your face. Dance with joy as it dampens
this dry place.

While looking to heaven on this rare rainy
day, pray that it will keep falling and falling
on this blessed day.

The Player

He appeared at the clubhouse dressed like a pro,
with his glove sticking out his rear pocket, all
set to go.

He paid his green fee and adjusted his hat
and walked out of the clubhouse and straight to
the starter's shack.

His clubs were waiting for him, neatly loaded
on his cart.
So he wasted no time telling everyone
he was ready to start.

He noticed he was one of four that he had
played with before, so with a smile he thought
he would turn in the lowest score.

After hitting his ball in the rough on number
one, he just blamed it on the sun. Two,
three, and four were about the same. The way
he was playing was an awful shame.

By the time he got to number eight, he was ready to
throw his clubs in the lake. It all happened so
quickly, from number one to eight. But with ten
holes to go, maybe it was not too late.

I was told that when he returned to the clubhouse
to post his score, he was very calm and left
with a bit of charm. He came like a pro and departed
like a pro.
But he left everyone wondering, *"where did his clubs go?"*

The Baby

Nestled in my mother's arms, free from care,
protected from harm, listening to her heart—
Oh! What a beautiful song.

I am not opening my eyes to see who else is near.
Instead let me find another position, a foot there,
an arm here, maybe my head just a bit near.

I heard someone say my daddy is waiting for me
to open my eyes. I shouldn't keep him waiting, but
mom just started another lullaby.

With the sound of her voice and the rhythm of her
heart, it's so hard for me to open my eyes so dad
can play his part. But when I'm in his arms and listening
to his heart, I hear him sing sometimes;
let's hope he doesn't start.

My New Bag

When the cell phone rang
I gave it no thought; I reached
into the pocketbook I'd just bought.

Still driving with one hand one the wheel
and the other in the pocketbook
an officer pulled me over
like I was a big time crook.

Now what did I do that was all that bad,
except trying to locate my cell phone in my
newly bought bag.

With the window down, and sitting erect,
I braced myself for the full effect.

He approached my car with book in hand
and had that same darn smile I saw
on Mickey's face at Disneyland.

Shanghai Volunteers

They were the sons and daughters
of Shanghai's best, who put true
love to the test.

Every morning, with smiles
on their faces, they returned
to their appointed places.

How can we forget what they
have done? Without them, the
games would not have been fun.

The Shanghai volunteers
gladly showed up every day
to get us to and from the games
without delay.

Coaches, staff, and athletes from
all over the world will remember these
volunteers as if they were precious
Chinese pearls.

Note: Written in honor of the volunteers in Shanghai, China that assisted at the 2007 World Games held for athletes with intellectual disabilities.

The Nightly Hunt

Like a hungry cat after prey, she must
stay in the hunt, not allowing any to get away.

The streets are so dark, but the corners are bright.
So to catch her prey, she must remain there
in the light.

Soon the prey will appear out of the dark, driving
really slow; she must move quickly; it must not
be allowed to go.

When she stepped into his world and was told
what he wanted, she become the prey, no longer
in charge of the hunt.

Night after night, the prey and the hunter
play this dangerous game, keeping alive the oldest
hunt that always ends in pain.

A Journey East

They flew to the Far East on a journey in time
to join other athletes to become one in body
and mind.

The goals they seek may not bring victory, but
none will come and go without making history.
When they assemble in Shanghai Stadium to
take their places, angels in heaven will make
a golden notation.

Before returning home, whence they came,
they should have met numerous
friends and obtained great fame.

What other group do you know of that can leave
and return as champions, other than
our wonderful Olympians.

Note: Written in honor of all the athletes from the United States that participated in the 2007 World Games held in Shanghai, China for athletes with intellectual disabilities.

Darkness

The darkness will soon be coming,
blocking those things that were
once clear and sunny.

There will be a chill in the air,
spreading all about, making the darkness
feel fearful and full of fright.

You won't see it coming because its way
is never clear; you must be on guard as it
approaches near.

Some will have enough light to see the way
clear, but many others will stumble and fall
in fear.

What are you doing to brighten your way
when the cloud of darkness comes on that
unclear day?

Will your light be bright enough
for you to see clear, showing there's
nothing in the darkness for you to fear?

Jena 6 (Louisiana)

It's hard to believe in this day and age
that racial hatred still has the nerve
to raise its ugly head.

Blacks and whites are beaten, and their
towns are torn apart; how on earth was
this allowed to start?

Although sadly it happened in the South,
is this sickness all about?

Imagine returning home after fighting
for the Land Of the Free and being told
you are not welcome to sit under this darn tree.

We are spending millions attempting
to communicate with outer space;
will they be warned of this racial hate?

Blacks and whites alike have marched and died
to rid us of this shame, but now in this day and age
we must sadly reflect on these words and
whence they came: "Free at last, free at last,
thank God almighty, we are free at last."

Now the question remains, with a great deal of pain.
Are we?

Shanghai

Shanghai, Shanghai with your buildings so tall,
let the sun come through; daylight calls.

Your children will soon be awake and will want to
play to get ready for World Games day.

All Shanghai will want to know how they will do
in swimming, running, or golf, just to name a few.

Many will be there from all over this great land
to cheer when they take the victory stand.

Shanghai, Shanghai, quickly push away the clouds;
let the sun come through. We want your children
to be the best at what they are about to do.

Note: Written in honor of all the Chinese athletes that participated in the 2007 World Games held for athletes with intellectual disabilities.

A Dog's Tail

There was a dog who thought he lost his tail.

He asked the duck, but got just a quack;
he then asked a beaver, who said, "I'm busy,
but I'll be right back."

Without an answer from his friends,
he felt this must be the end. Depressed
and saddened by the thought of losing his tail,
he jumped the fence and ran up the trail.

He met a man selling tails,
but with no money, there wasn't a sale.

He ran to the river to end it all,
but the reflection from the water
showed he hadn't lost his tail at all.

Let's Play

Look at all these things: climbing bars,
a merry-go-round, and swings.
Don't just stand there, let's go play.
You think we have all day?

But before we play, let me tell you
a few things. The swings are okay,
but the sliding board gets so hot
you can fry fish right there, on the spot.

Be careful when you roll and play in the grass.
grownups come here at night and make
noise and break glass. Also, don't play in the sand.
The stuff the dogs leave, you don't want to touch
with your hands.

You see all that stuff written all about?
Don't try to read it; it's something called graffiti.
I don't know what it's supposed to say;
it keeps getting painted over, but it's right back
the next day.

Well, let's go play and try to have fun and not think
of all the bad stuff someone's done.
We better hurry; the baby is awake and mom's off the
cell phone, and soon she'll be calling for us to go home.

Places to Go

You ever wonder where your dog goes when
he's asleep?

You think he goes to China to climb
the Great Wall or hops a train to New York
to leap over Niagara Falls?

Maybe he doesn't go anywhere but stays
right there at home to keep an eye on his
favorite bone.

He will never tell where he's been, but you know
he had fun; just look at that grin.

Tonight when I go to sleep, I'm going to have fun too.
I'm going to Disneyland and the San Diego
Zoo.

When I wake in the morning and he sees the grin on my face,
He will wonder too, *Where has she been,*
for goodness' sake?

My Sister Dorothy

I have a sister that I want you all to know
because she's such a sweet person
and you can't help but love her so.

I believe that when God made her, he may
have broken the mold, because you will
be hard pressed to find another
with such a heart of gold

Although she's been ill for such a long
time, you would never know it, because
she never complains or whines.

What a wonderful sister she's always
been; the old stork would be hard pressed
to bring a mom and dad such a sweet child again.

I'm deeply sorry I can't visit her
but once a year, but by sending
cards and letters and calling her by
phone, I try to keep her near.

For those of you who haven't met her,
do so before it's too late, because when God
calls her home, she's going through the
Precious Children's Gate.

The Appointment

When we walked into the office, there was a chill in the air,
and there sat the dentist's chair.

When she went with the dentist to take her seat,
I was sure happy they were not my teeth.

Soon the sound of the drill had me on the edge of my seat,
and from where I sat, I could see her feet.

She wore open-toe shoes that day,
and I could see her toes slowly curling up a ways.

With the sound of the drill and the hissing of air,
I then saw her feet slowly rising in the air.

Soon I could hear moans and screams,
and then I saw the wildest leg-kicking I had ever seen.

After what seemed like an hour, the drilling stopped,
And I saw her toes uncurl and her legs slowly drop.

After a moment's pause, she appeared at the door,
holding a new toothbrush in her hand,
and without a word or smile, we left the same way we came.

When the Time Comes

Many of us have lost close friends,
family members, mothers, and fathers.

Tomorrow was not promised,
and we should understand it so,
realizing that just like our loved ones,
tomorrow may be our time to go.

The loved ones we lost were not here
for us to own; they were all children
belonging to the Heavenly Father,
and the Father decided to call them home.

Now, if you are a child of the Father,
you should understand what's been said and
never ever think of your loved ones as being dead.

They are alive in our hearts and minds
for us to always call near, and when the
Heavenly Father calls us home, we will
again see them clear.

Dwelling daily on self-pity, sadness, and sorrow
will not solve a thing. Be of great joy, and thankful
that you are also a child of the King.

Madness

Why do they spray all over the place?
It's so ugly and shows lack of taste.

With paint red, purple, black, or green,
are they that desperate to be seen?

They must not be proud of what they display,
otherwise it would be done during the day.

Everywhere you look, without respect
for property, you, or me; we are exposed
to this ugly graffiti.

You think there is an illness that
blinds them from this shame,
preventing them from seeing
their real hurt and pain.

You can't help but see it on walls,
buildings, and trucks, and I'm sure
you will agree that this mess is a total disgust.

All Grown Up

Now our daughter is off to college to pursue her goal;
can anyone believe she's really this old?

I guess we all knew this moment in time
would appear;
God knows we will miss our little dear.

It's no more "clean your room, stop the noise,"
or "Put away your toys. It's now,
"watch out for those college boys."

Her little brother can use the computer
all he pleases, but sadly, she won't
be here for him to tease.

We are all so glad; we loved her so much each day,
and we pray our love will strengthen her
while she's away.

Now it's down to business; worldly things must wait.
All that matters now is her graduation date.

The Neighborhood

It so sad when a neighborhood dies.
At one time mothers joyfully cooked,
children played, and babies cried.

The empty houses are so still and cold.
I wonder what happened to all those goals.

I wonder who were the first to go
and, those that left just to follow the flow?

It's so sad when a neighborhood dies.
The abandoned buildings seem to cry out in pain,
with their shutters closed as if to hide the shame.

I was away when my neighborhood died.
Wasn't there to see the first to go
and those that followed the flow.

I remember the happy times way back then,
but sadly this neighborhood, too,
will never rise again.

Moving Forward

Running. Running from pain and despair,
but not just anywhere. The night is so dark,
but I can still see the star that's leading me afar.

I must keep moving; I can hear the sounds of
the hounds as my thoughts guide me,
northbound.

I'll need help along the way; I must remember
those safe places where I was told to stay.

If I'm caught and returned whence I came,
I'll be stripped, beaten, and driven to pain.

I must not look back; there is nothing there
for me to see. I must keep looking
forward, forward; dear God, I must be free.

The Cell Phone

Fumbling for the cell phone is driving me insane.
I'd better get over in the right-hand lane.

Looking straight ahead, not wanting to be unsafe;
where is that cell phone, for goodness' sake?

At last I found it between the seats,
but by then there was no Beethoven; not so much as a beep.

I quickly looked to see who had called,
but I didn't recognize the number at all.

Red lights flashing from the rear
and those hand gestures from passing motorists
Oh, dear.

I pulled to the curb and came to a stop,
and wouldn't you know it? It's the same smiling cop.

The Golfer

A three-hundred-yard drive was nothing for him;
even chipping to the greens was just a fine trim.

But when it came to putting, that was another story.
There was something mysterious between him and glory.

When he struck the ball to make the putt,
the dear ball again went amuck.

On bended knees with head bowed in pure sorrow,
he very quietly said,

"Dear God, please be with me tomorrow."

The Fly

There was a fly in my soup,
trying to eat the beans;
such a sight I have never seen.

As he held on to the corn to stay afloat,
he opened his mouth and began to choke.

As I watched the poor fly gasping for air
my soup was getting cold, plus beans,
corn, and juice were being flung everywhere.

How he got there I can only guess,
but wherever he came from,
there will be one fly less.

Fat Cat

This cat was in the kitchen, looking with a stare
at a mouse with a sophisticated flair.

He circled the mouse to get a better look,
but the mouse slid away like a smooth running brook.

The temper rose within the cat, but the mouse thought
he was safe, because this cat was way too fat.

The mouse started dancing to his hole, acting cool,
thinking, *no problem; this cat's a fool.*

I understood his thoughts that day, but it's a shame
he didn't see the broom coming from the other way.

Time Flies

If time flies, then tell me, please,
on what day does it leave?

I'm really happy where I stand,
but I heard there's free candy in Wonderland.

I hope the trip won't take too long;
it would be sad if it's all gone.
Packing a few things would be a breeze:
an apple, an orange, even some crackers
and cheese.

Do you think my mom would be very mad
if I took one of her good plastic bags?

Why, I could fill it to the top,
and we could eat candy till we popped.

Oh, please tell me on what day time flies;
if you don't, I'll surely cry.

I'm sure the trip isn't free,
but how much can the price
be for a little girl just three?

Military Daughter's Prayer

Dear Father up above, please return quickly;
we need your love.

Churches are on every corner, and missionaries
praise you in song, but it doesn't seem to
stop all the wrong.

Hunger and war abound everywhere, but
world leaders just don't seem to care.

I know you said "free will" and that it is up to
man, but please hurry as fast as you can.

I'm just a child, but help me understand
why so many are dying in far-off lands.

My mom is hugging my best friend's mother with
a letter in her hand, and if it's like the one mom got,
I fear she won't be seeing her dad again.

Some People

Some people will come with smiles
others will come with a bit of rain,
but the ones you should watch out
for, are those that come with pain.

They really don't care about you or
those before, there seem to be no
meaning to their life, nor joy.

It's no use trying to change their ways
it's best to let them pass, because if you
allow their pain to enter your heart
there it will last.

I bet you can think of one or two that
have tried to hurt you in some way.
If this is so, then you understand there's
nothing more to say.

Who is an American

Who is an American; it's hard to see,
so many are here today just for the liberty.
Unaware of the price that's been paid
by those that were free, and those who
were slaves.

I know it's more than just waving the flag
or making a lot of noise on July the Fourth.
So to answer who is an American, I must
give it some thought.

An American to me can be of any ethnicity,
but must have one thing in common
and that's to be free. Willing to pay the price
that must be paid, to keep America and its
people free, and not enslaved.

Respecting the land and all its wonder, willing
to fight if necessary come hell or thunder.
Showing an understanding to those who are new,
and have proven they also respect the red, white,
and blue.

Signs of the Times

People watching can be such fun as they hurry
to finish this or that before the day is done.
Ladies walking by in tight jeans, smiling as they
do so, aware they have been seen.

Young men passing by in baggy pants exposing
their underwear in total disgust, with heavy
chains around their necks, which would lay a
pack mule in the dust.

Little children smiling as if aware their parents will
do anything to avoid a fuss, as they lead the poor
souls into Toys "R" Us.

Young girls walking by in flip flops looking twice
their age, with bodies developed far beyond their stage.
Exposing body parts that should be against the law; but
than again, it's nothing I haven't seen before.

All that I have seen today I could have taken in stride,
but when grandma strolled by wearing all those
tattoos; it was time to say goodbye.

Blame Ted

Well I better get up and head downstairs.
It's awful quiet in the house without Ted.
I'll have a quick cup of coffee and a slice
of bread; load my golf clubs, to heck with
making up the bed.

The day is waiting; the sky is bright and clear.
 After my round of golf, I'll have a few beers.
Then I'll return home and I'll take off everything right
down to my shoes, pop another beer and shoot
some pool.

When the sun goes down and all the neighbors are
asleep, I'll get out one of the cars and burn some rubber
in the street. When the cops come over and ask me if I'm
out of my head, I'll say don't blame me, blame Ted.

Choir Member

Sadness and sorrow is present once again.
The Heavenly Father called home another
kin.

She'll be remembered for many years
to come. It was so sad that she had to
be the one.

I wonder if she will be asked to join the
Heavenly Choir, to greet other kinfolk who
will be along in the sweet bye and bye.

If so, let's hope another Kin isn't called
none too soon.

As sweet and lovely as she was, she
informed me some time ago she
couldn't carry a tune.

Come What May

The news that I received at Christmas time
caused sadness, fear and anger to rush
through my mind. Why me I thought, what did I do
to deserve this bad news.

Did I do something wrong? I am a loving person
who takes no pleasure in seeing others harmed.
I help when needed and ask nothing in return. So
why had this sad news come?

I called on the Father and asked him why and
he said fear not my son and dry your eyes. We
have been together for over seventy-two years,
so why all of a sudden do you now fear?

I apologized and asked for forgiveness. I felt
ashamed for thinking He was not there, fully aware
of the burden I bear. Sadness, fear and anguish
thoughts have all but gone away. Things are looking
much brighter, and I am ready to face come what may.

Curtains Drawn

All the curtains were drawn; the room was nearly dark
as family members sat about making small talk.
It happened so suddenly. Warning signs never appeared.
He seemed to have been so healthy throughout the year.

It seems to happen this way so many times to yours and mine.
There is no answer when death comes, just another heavy burden
to be shared one by one. It will affect each one in a different way.
Some will cry, some will deny, while others pray.

But whatever we do to lessen the pain we must one day reopen
the curtains again, allowing the sunlight back in. While standing
there feeling the sun as it shines thought your window glass,
pray that it will be strong enough to melt away all the grief and
sadness within at last.

Forgiveness

Making his way across the desert that was well
over a hundred and fifteen degrees. Super dry
no breeze, and of course no trees. The heat
was too much and before long he was on his
hands and knees.

One of the buzzers asked, should we help him along?
The other buzzers rolled in the sand laughing, pointing
and wondering who in the world invited this rookie along.

Now the guy there on his hands and knees
said to the buzzers he was offended. He lectured
them about their insensitivity and their unwarranted
humor.

Feeling ashamed about all their laughter and humor,
the buzzers ask the guy his forgiveness should
there be a funeral.

Fort Hood

Several were killed in a place called
Fort Hood. Killed by a solider not easily
understood who was also a member
of their brotherhood.

Why did he inflict such needless harm?
What drove him to do such a horrible
thing to his very own? Were the signs there
but those closest failed to say, because it was
not the brotherhood's way?

Shot dead not knowing why, they were not
prepared to tell their love ones goodbye.
They never had that chance where they sat
and stood, when shot by a deranged solider
in a place called Fort Hood.

Friends

Since her friend had gone sadness filled each day.
As she passed looking at his house, she hoped
the front door would open and he would step out.

When they were kids they would play for hours
running about flying model airplanes or on their
knees in the dirt driving toy trucks. Laughing and
joking calling each other funny names until their
stomachs ached in pain.

Remembering those days and the fun they shared
she slowly bowed her head and softly quietly said.
Please Father when I look at his house tomorrow
let him be there.

Get moving

Up and at it to start my day. Entire world, places to play. Maybe climb a mountain, run a race, or go fishing at my favorite place.

But I feel so comfortable between these warm blankets and sheets. It wouldn't take much to roll over to get a wee bit more sleep.

Wow! Look at the sun, rising slowly in the east, as if pulling at my feet. If I don't get up now the morning will pass me by and I will wonder, *"what if"* under a dark sky.

Heavenly Shade

I watched the sunlight fade
as Mother Nature lowered
her heavenly shade.

Lower and lower her heavenly
shade is drawn, until all light
was gone.

Some will sleep peacefully while
others may lie awake fearful that
they will not see the dawn.

During the light all things seem
certain and clear. What is it about
the darkness that causes moments
of wonder and or fear?

Little Grace

Once again, today I was able to see
the sunshine and saw so many smiles
before bedtime.

I pray tomorrow will be the same, while
dreaming of puppy dogs, ice cream
and sugar canes.

Memorial Day

On this day when so many of our brave men
and women in their graves lay,
few are taking the time to say thanks
with a single flag display.

On my street alone with so many homes.
I can count only two flags to honor those
brave souls now resting on heaven's throne.

Is it because they don't understand its
meaning or just don't care? Or is it all
about enjoying a three day weekend
thanks to those laying there.

They may be dead to some, but never to me
because thanks to them this Country and its
people are free. When neighbors drive by and
see my flag on display, I hope they will take the
time to reflect why I honor our fallen dead
on this Memorial Day.

Merry Christmas

It's the end of October and you
wouldn't believe the number
of artificial Christmas trees I see.

Tall ones, short ones of all different colors
to buy. Some fully decorated with
Bugs Bunny Daffy Duck and Popeye.

Now what do they have to do with Christmas?
Your guess is as good as mine.
I guess as the young folks say,
"I need to get with the times."

Not fit

Dead bodies were thrown on the highway,
some missing heads, arms, legs and hands
all in the name of Meth and or cocaine that
will kill or drive users insane.

The dead were men and children, mothers with
unborn babies still inside. Thrown there by a
drug cartel to show the world they have no
respect for life, or fear of hell. It's all about
protecting the garbage they sell.

This isn't the first time nor will it be the last
that such a senseless tragedy has come to pass.
It's all about money, greed and power by people
with deranged minds who aren't fit to live in your
world or mine.

One Brave Soul

There are no tattoos metal clips, or pins
on my body as you can see. I have no complaints
about how God made me.

He made my hair a bit short and thick,
my eyes brown, and my skin like fine dark
coffee from my head to the ground.

There are those who may say if your hair isn't
naturally straight and your eyes are not
gray or blue, God somehow made a mistake
when he made you.

Now that is a terrible thing to say about God
the Father of us all. I often wonder just where
do some people get the nerve to make such a call?

Telling the Heavenly Father he made a mistake
is mighty brave. What do you think his reply would
be when they ask to be saved?

Poor Fellow

When she smiled, turned her back
to him and walked away, nothing else
needed to be said that day.

He tried to ask for forgiveness but
could not find the right words in time.
Once again his heart failed to persuade his
mind.

Another relationship lost because he
failed to recognize true love and trust.

Show A little Love

The little bush does not ask for much, just a little water
 a few times a month, just enough to keep him alive
and prevent the dreaded slump.

He is a desert plant and knows he can withstand
just about anything under the sun; except
careless hikers who roam in the desert just for fun.

The Box

Holding her hand while making small talk,
wondering how he would break the news.
He slowly removed his hand and turned
to face her close. She could see from his
expression he wasn't about to tell her a joke.

He slowly reached into his coat pocket
and took out a little box. She could see that it
was way too small to hold a watch.
A chill ran down her spine and goose
bumps appeared on her arms.
She braced herself for the question she's
been waiting to hear for so long.

When he opened the box to show her
what was there, she took one look, screamed
to high heaven and jumped up onto a chair.
It was the most beautiful ring she had ever
seen. Nothing would come close, not in her
wildness dreams.

While on the chair still screaming, she first
let down her hair and loosened her blouse.
He just stood there dumb founded and
in shock and dropped the box.

She then dove off the chair hoping to land
in his arms, but she figured wrong.
He had stepped to one side to recover
the box that he had dropped.

The Delay

Helen they should be here in just a few. Please
don't allow this to worry you.
If they were delayed along the way, I'm sure
they would call to say.

Yet they may have tried to call, but were
not able to get through. You know in certain
locations what cell phones will do.
You must be patient and not think the worst.

Here you see, I'll get the phone, it's probably them
not far from home.

Hello? You are where? She did what in the car?
When? No way, you say. I'll inform her.
Helen my dear, you have two more grandchildren I fear.

The Miner

His face was dirty; his body was tired.
He looked old. His mind yearned for the
daylight above as he labored in the mine
deep below.

It was a dangerous job, but he had to do it
come what may, because his family had to
be cared for and bills he had to pay.

When the mine exploded, the earth shook above.
His wife cried aloud, dear God do not let it be my love.
But it was her love. God rest his soul deep,
underground covered with coal.

Like his father and grandfather before him, the mine
was always the way. So like them, he also chose
this way to earn his pay.

Thinking it would be just for a little while and then
he would be on his way. But the years passed by
quickly and by then he knew no other way. Now
there in the darkness deep, his dead body lay.

The Sound

If I were to climb over these walls hoping
to be free, how long would it be before this
side of the walls again I would see?
Where would I run? Which direction would
I go? Who among those still left behind would
tell them so?

My body and mind are in so much pain.
The repeated pounding of the hammers
are slowly driving me insane. The singing
by fellow inmates I can no longer stand to hear.
There is no way I'll survive another year.

Through it all I can still hear the sound of the
judge's gavel and the words he said to me that day,
"Young man for this crime you will surely pay."

Before being taken away, I turned to look for my mother
but she was nowhere to be found. But painfully
I heard in the distance, a familiar tearful
sound.

The Trip

Green sky, purple butterflies another
midnight lullaby. Soft breeze he feels
while floating here and there, reaching
out to touch nightly stars with loving care.

Deeper and deeper he floats into the night.
Guided seemingly by a thousand beautiful
flowers and flashing lights. As he passes the
Milky Way, Jupiter and Mars, he begins to wonder;
if this trip has taken him too far.

The Way

You need not worry about what's ahead because God will be with you. Trust in Him and be not afraid.

Even if the way becomes dark, He will light the way. Just remember to follow His instructions, and not what others say.

He will never turn His back on you. You must never think so. He will be with you always as you go.

Do the best that you can. Don't worry about what others may say. God is the one, not man, who will show you the way.

Whatever it takes

Candidates will go about smiling
and shaking hands, joyfully kissing babies
and giving speeches throughout the land.

When campaigning in the South they will
dress up in bib coveralls, and if need be,
take part in a barroom brawl.

Out West they will spit and shoot the bull.
Even ride the meanest steer without spilling
a drop of beer.

If voters don't seem to be buying their show
out comes their backup, tons of dough. They have
no shame about the price. They are on the road
to the White House.

You Never Know

I'm told the sky is falling, but I'm not
worried because I have my umbrella
in hand. Actually, my only concerns are
should I venture outside, and where is a good
place to stand?

I'm not concerned about the clouds because
they always look soft and fluffy as they
float and sway. Sometimes objects
appear in them making beautiful displays.

It's difficult to tell if the sky is really falling
because it's such a bright and beautiful day.
But to be on the safe side, I should open my
umbrella. What do you say?

Young Tongue

The adult felt quite at ease socializing with the young, until they spoke in a strange tongue.

When he asked one of the young, was there something wrong? The young said, *"S"mofo butter layin me to da'Bone! Jackin' me up . . . tight! Me.*

Somewhat taken back, he quietly said to another of the young, I don't understand the young man's tongue. She quickly said you ain't the only one. *"Jive dude don't got no brains any how! Hmmph.*

A Bite Out Of Crime

The house was located on a hilltop majestic and
pristine. The owner was proud of his house and
wanted to make sure it was seen.

He surrounded it with beautiful bushes and trees
plus a gorgeous lawn, and made sure it was all well
protected by a state of the art burglar alarm.

One night a thief from the hood climbed the hill
to steal what he could, but not able to get by the alarm
so there he stood. He then sat on the lawn next to the house
to figure things out that dark night.

There on the lawn overlooking the lights below he
laid back to allow his thoughts to flow. As he laid
there wondering what he should do next, the sprinkler
system came on and got him all wet.

When he sat up to move, he felt a warm breath on the back
of his neck. He slowly turned to see what was there and
low and behold, there stood a very large dog to add to his despair.

To this day when neighbors walk by the house on the hilltop
looking so pristine, they are reminded of that dark night, and
those awful horrifying screams.

A New Day

Over a million strong standing arm and arm, excited about what was to come after waiting so long. Everyone wanted to be close when Obama took the oath, but just being there was enough for most.

They came from all corners of this great land, and stood for hours in freezing temperatures with cold feet and hands just to get a glimpse of Obama, when he raised his right hand.

Joyful tears and smiles were the order of the day, differences laid at bay. Who among the millions would dare spoil such an honorable day, as red, yellow, black, and white, glorified in this day in history after such a long hard fight.

At Day's End

Another note telling me what's
been set aside for my dinner and
what time they will be home.

I should have run into the night,
they wouldn't have noticed that
I was gone.

It's the same thing day after day.
I feel so sad in this house all alone,
as if my parents just dropped
me off after bringing me home.

I fear the night, so here I will stay,
hoping and praying once again
they will spend time with me at
the end of the day.

Baby Power

Sometimes I wonder if another poem
will ever form, and then a baby will pass
by in their mother's arm, and my heart will
begin to warm.

What a beautiful message they seem to send,
awakening my thoughts, and that of my pen.
Although quickly passing, and it was just a
glimpse, the message sent was more then
a hint.

They seem to know actually what they are doing,
when they flash those warm beautiful smiles, as if
knowing of my problem, or that I haven't written
a poem in a while.

What is it about a baby's smile that seems to capture
and warm our hearts. It places them in a world of
their own, majestically apart. Their smile can brighten
any dark day, even cause grown-ups to start making
funny sounds, and want to play.

If only they knew of the power they possess, they could
take over the world. But not being able to change their
diapers on their own, it's best to leave that thought
alone.

So let us accept the smiles, and or the hints they gladly give,
and keep it a secret about the power they possess, and let
their moms control the rest.

Choosing

Take note when choosing a lover if she must
be as pretty as a lovely rose, or that he be as tall
and majestic like the great oak tree. Or stylish with
a Ph.D.

When picking a rose be careful of the thorns,
if not picked carefully blood may be drawn.

A tree, no matter how majestic and tall, if
deprived of water it will one day fall.

Stylish or not, without common sense, that
Ph.D is of no value at all.

Crumbs

Oh, dear! Here he comes, looking for crumbs, walking lightly trying not to make a scene, as he munches away sipping tea in between. What nerve. He seems to have no fear of man or bird.

I would never swat the little bug, or do him any harm. He always appears with a smile, laying on the charm. Although I should warn him, my wife may not be amused, so I hope he can handle this bit of news.

She won't allow him to wash down the crumbs with a sip of her tea, so I hope he will understand, but no doubt he will come to this realization quickly, should he find himself flattened in the palm of her hand.

Her Light

I find myself staring so many times and wonder
if she's aware of the bright light she shines? I'm
amazed how peaceful and calm she always seem
to be, totally relaxed totally free.

She has given me her heart with no strings attached
asking little of me to give back. But I have given her my
undying love throughout these years. Although from
time to time it may not appear.

No, I'm not a flawless husband and probably wouldn't
win the husband of the year, but I love her dearly,
and the thought of losing her has always been my
greatest fear.

We been married for a very long time and I wouldn't
have it any other way. I'm a lucky man to have
married such a beautiful lady that has shined so brightly
day after day.

Her Mary

One minute I may be standing there,
the next minute I may be gone.
I never know when angels will take
me in their loving arms.

But one thing is for sure in Heaven,
I will proclaim near and far, of all the
daughters back on earth my Mary
is the best of them all.

Hurricane Kate

She will be spinning out of the south like
hell on wheels, bent on destroying and making
no deals. Don't be fooled just because her
name is Kate; I would advise you to pack quickly,
for your life may be at stake.

Now if you are aware of a number
she's been assigned, like a three, four or five
don't waste time turning off the stills or
hugging the livestock, just wave as you
say goodbye.

Do not get any strange ideas when Kate turns
off all the lights, she just sparing you the agony
of not seeing all your stuff fly by in flight.

Things are going to be a mess for a while,
Kate is not fooling around. Folks leaving told
me she has already tore up half the town.

Now hurry and get grandma and grandpa,
and Old Blue in the car. As you pass by the
still, fill a fruit jar of your very best, old Blue
appears to be weakening, and may need a sip
or two due to all the stress.
Now get going, and God Bless.

It's All Free

Shame on you South Africa. Shame on you all
for turning a deaf ear to your women and young
girl's call. Rape is known throughout the
African land. How in Heaven's name can you do
nothing, and allow this degrading act to stand.

A little girl of six is taken, and raped for two days long,
and you give the impression that it's no big deal, just
another note added to your long list of sad
songs. Where are your leaders, don't they care.
Don't they understand this crime they share?

These acts of rape are not isolated cases that occur
every now and then, these are acts performed daily
by men who know they can. Your wildlife is well protected
so visitors can pay to see, but your women and young girls
are not protected, so they are abused by your men, and it's
all free.

Judy

What can I say about Judy, the youngest
of us all, she was a chubby little baby and
wasn't even tall.

I remember Mom would dress her up pretty
and all, but I never remember Judy ever playing
jump rope or step ball.

Then one day Mom and Judy were gone.
I was a little guy, and at the time didn't know
why. Sister Judy and I never had a chance to say
goodbye.

Through the years, I would see her off and on,
but by then she was all grown. I always felt sad
that we didn't get to know each other back then
at home.

She is gone again with Mom and her sister Dorothy
to admire their heavenly wings and all, and I bet
they are driving the angels crazy, bragging who's
the best at jump rope and step ball.

Killing and Hate

Sometimes, I believe some men were sent
here from some place deep in outer space,
because they feared them, and sent them adrift
to save themselves before it was too late.

After arriving here on earth, it appeared that it did
not take them long to start spreading their seeds
of killing and hate, that sadly dictated both animal
and human fate.

Killing and hating seem to give them great power
and joy. They even teach children at an early age
how to kill through the use of games and hand-
held toys.

Why do they act that way, what drives them on? Seemingly
there's no limit to the way they contrive to inflict pain
or do harm. If you know the answer please tell me. I
would like to hear, because like those that sent them
adrift, we too should begin to fear.

My Sister Winnie

I heard a laughter from her that came from deep
inside, a laughter that took me quite by surprise.

The tears that appeared I did not try to contain,
because her laughter was telling me, that she too
had broken the chain that had held her pain.

The death of her husband, plus our mother and sister,
had affected us all in body and mind, so I knew the healing
process for each of us would come at different times.

To hear her laugh so joyful and free was telling me,
she at last found the key.

No Ordinary Bird

A little bird settled in the tree outside my
window carrying a piano and what appeared
to be a song book under his other wing. You will
agree, this was no ordinary thing.

When he sat down at the piano and opened
his book, I thought he was going to sing.
Instead this little bird played the wildest jazz
on that piano that I had never heard.

Just then, other birds began to settle in the tree,
but showed no signs of amazement, like me.

Then the bird at the piano switched from jazz
to the blues, and in a matter of seconds all
the other birds in the tree started rocking,
even before the bird at the piano had gotten into
his groove.

I figured these birds must have come up from
the south, around New Orleans way, and stopped
in the tree outside my window, to let off a bit of stress,
before continuing north that day.

I'm glad he stopped by my window. What
an extraordinary bird. Too bad, I did not
record it all, to prove to you what I had seen
and heard. Darn good jazz and blues played
by no ordinary bird.

No Strings Attached

So full of life so full of joy this little
girl this little boy. They play with such
freedom with no strings attached, letting
each joyful moment pass never looking back.

When did it happen, at what age; what
were the moments what did I trade? It
definitely was not for love of money, or that
of fame, so where can I place the blame?

I think it was all about age and I just felt
ashamed. But today, I can care less about age
blame or shame. I am kicking off my shoes
and getting in the game.

I know I will be sore in the morning because
my granddaughter Grace just jumped in my
chest, and my grandson Bryce got me in a
headlock but I could care less. I haven't had this
much fun in years. I hope they don't stop just
because of my tears.

Open Arms

Sorry you did not meet her before it was too late.
She left some time ago to meet angels at the
precious children's gate. I bet there was a
welcome fit for a queen; such a divine celebration
that Heaven had never seen.

Roses thrown about, trumpeters playing sweet angelic
tunes over and over throughout the morning past
noon. I bet Dorothy just smiled, and didn't say a word, she
just listened as the head angel read off the welcoming
words.

We welcome you home Dorothy after waiting so long.
The Heavenly Father is waiting for you with open arms.
We know your love ones will miss you back on earth
and the Heavenly Father fully understands their hurt.

But your work there was done, and now it's time for you
to rest. You did well and were one of our best. But don't
get too comfortable, because there are family members
here to greet you too; your father, your mother, plus Aunt
Hattie, and Aunt Sue just to name a few.

Our Friend Joe

There is a man of the hour.
There is power in every hour.
The power is "the word" for
all those who have heard.
Poetry is the power, the man
of the hour is Joe.

Note: This little poem was written by Mary Zollinger our neighbor, and the pretty little card it was written on was designed by her daughter Elizabeth. Mary's husband Dennis presented it to me Christmas morning 2008.

Pondering

Every time I reach a mountaintop and sit
and look over this great land, I sometimes
wonder why in heavens name anyone would
leave all that I see in man's hand.

When I walk through the valleys below,
I notice destruction everywhere.
If only he would sit where I now sit
maybe he would understand.

The forests are being damaged from over
cutting of the trees; lakes and rivers are
drying up, plus the air is polluted as far as the
eye can see. Why man doesn't get it, is
beyond me.

Some people seem to think it's no big deal
because their money or the government will
eventually correct all the wrong that has been
done.

Plus, Mother Nature should understand that
mankind is just trying to improve his living
standards, and at the same time, having a
bit of fun.

Pure Adrenaline

Don't try to guess their age, most likely you
will guess wrong the people that show up at the
recreation center on Tuesday nights are young
at heart *"Line Dancers"*, and ready to *"Step"* if
necessary all night long.

I don't go with my wife, I just send her on her way
but I hear there's a lot of fancy *"Stepping"* and
"Swirling" that's not often seen, with very little rest
in between.

I'm told the music they dance to is fast with a heck of
a beat, so the AC is set very low to control their heat.
Those screams I'm told you hear from them every
now and then are not screams of pain, they occur when
they reached their peak, and running on pure adrenaline.

Read Me a Poem

Read me a poem daddy. Read me a poem
before your words fade away. Oh dear God,
let him speak again I pray.

Why didn't I listen before when he wanted
to share; goodness knows it wasn't much
for me to bear. Read me a poem daddy,
while I hold you near.

Hurry dear father before the angels take you
away I fear. I remembered you wanted to
read me the poem, The Light of Day.
Read me this poem please, I promise you
this time I will now stay.

Respect

A dog walked by a few feet away and lifted
his leg to leave his mark. I then wondered
who sprayed graffiti on the wall across the
street during the dark?

I'm sitting here looking at a newly built wall
and before the cement even dried, some
sad soul figured during the night graffiti should
be applied.

We all know that dogs can't talk. To communicate
with other dogs they leave their mark. The sad
souls that spray graffiti I assume do the same. But
they, not like the dog, have become a full blown pain.

Of all the graffiti sprayed about, have you ever seen
the word, *"Respect"* painted anywhere, in red, purple
black or green? I doubt if you ever will. The word respect
don't seem to give these sad souls their required thrill.

School's Out

She pulled up in front of the school greeting
everyone with a toot of the horn while talking
on her cell phone.

She kept the engine running, while visualizing
her escape route, because yesterday she got boxed
in, and no way was it going to happen again.

When her child jumped in, and buckled up
she didn't say a word, but smiled as she slowly
pulled away from the curb.

There's an opening no time to waste, she jammed
on the gas and smiled as she heard her wheels spin.
But the smile soon faded, when her son informed her
she left the neighbor's kid again.

Shame

Brought to a country like animals in chains,
families split and sold like cattle by men without
shame. They were stripped of everything, even
their names. Beaten to submission should they
dare resist before removing their chains.

Sold as property to whoever could afford, or traded
like valuable coins to work in fields, or someone's home.
Held in bondage and disgrace; never knowing
their fate.

They began to hear of a God that their owner said
was kind and good, so they listened closely every chance
they could. They began to tell others of what they had
heard, and began practicing the owner's God's word.

Now at last they had something to cling to which gave
them hope, after hearing what the owner said
God spoke. Night after night they prayed to this
same God, asking him to free them and remove their
heavy yoke.

After years of pain, and suffering freedom did come, but was
it because of the owner's God, or that of a war and the power
of the gun? Human disgrace, brothers killing brothers,
all because of what a few shameful men started and done.

Should I or Shouldn't I

I always feel sad when I see them
standing there, heads bent in total despair,
holding a sign that indicates their needs
or the burden they bear.

I feel a bit uneasy, when one approaches my car,
and sometimes pretend and look afar.
The sign they carry sends mixed signals to my
brain. Should I or shouldn't I give a dollar or two,
and will it really lessen their pain?

I notice some have locations where they stand
each day, and often wonder if this is just another
scam or an easy payday? I also notice that they
are only allowed in certain parts of town, as if
the upper crust don't want to see them, or have
them roaming around.

I give to agencies that are helping the down and out,
but I have not quite made up my mind about the same
on street corners with signs depicting their pain, asking
for money while I wait for the light to change.

Sign and Initial Here

Procedural complication that may result, so
you must understand we must cover our butts.
Nothing to worry about, nothing new, many
have signed this form reluctantly, and watery
eyed, as you are about to do.

Look it over before you sign, just relax and
take your time. You notice it says stroke,
mini stroke, brain damage, loss of vision, heart
failure, rental damage, trauma, burns, loss of
limb, heart failure, organ damage, emotional
pain and suffering, and potential death, but
don't take too long, we must get on with your
stress test.

Therapeutic measures that may be necessary
to treat complications that may arise, we will do
everything to keep you alive. But are not limited
to: intravenous medications, blood transfusions,
mechanical ventilation and cardio version/ defibrillation.
Look it over and please sign and initial where the highlights
are, don't worry the injection needle won't
leave a scar.

So Very Far

Our young men and women are sent to war
where many have been killed. Those that sent
them there, continue to justify their deaths still.

There's something wrong with this picture that's
making it unclear. I'm not totally convinced
their deaths will assure or strengthen our liberty.

Don't get me wrong, I will always defend this
great land, but the daily deaths in Iraq or Afghanistan
is hard for me to except or comprehend.
When will it be over, there's still no indications that
peace is close at hand. It's said our leaders rushed
to war, and failed to formulate a victory or an end plan.

May God rest his hands on a mother and father who must
live with an everlasting scar, after learning their child was
killed in a strange land, so very far so very far.

Still Below

Not too deep below many of her crew still lay,
many unaware of what happened that Sunday.
An enemy came out of the sun with one thing
in mind, to do as much damage in the short
period of time.

There was little or no warning for those below
or time for them to react. The enemy above was
determined to press forward that Sunday morning
with their attack.

The morning was still, and the waters were calm
but the enemy quickly changed all of that and started
a firestorm. The storm was so devastating, bombs exploding
all about, several hitting a ship where her crew rested
below, and many were not able to get out.

The ship was the USS Arizona, and there at the bottom of
Pearl Harbor she still lay, with many of her crew inside to
this day. December the seventh 1941, is a day to remember
and Americans should never forget how her crew became
entombed in the bowels of this ship.

The Call

My mind began to wonder, my heart skipped a beat,
who in the world is calling at this dark hour, awaking
me from my sleep? Let it be a wrong number, Lord
I pray, spare me of any news that would darken or
cast a shadow over the coming light of day.

The ringing always seems louder than normal during
this time of night, adding to my nervousness and
heartfelt fright. Who can it be, what do they want,
I ask myself while fumbling for the phone all at
once.

I tried to be calm as I put the receiver to my ear, bracing
myself for what I'm about to hear. The voice was low
on the other end, words spoken I could barely
comprehend. I said speak up I can't hear you and don't
understand, but all I heard was a, *"click"*, in my ear,
and the darkness was still again.

The Day After

Trying to write a happy poem is not
an easy task these days, as countries
attack countries, people out of work,
mad suicide bombers on the loose,
businesses falling apart, plus people
losing their homes just to start.

The whole darn world seems to be out of
sync, as if not knowing where to go or
which way to turn, to find needed answers
from past lessons learned, as if locked in a
dark room endlessly roaming about, hoping
that someone will find the right key in time
to let them out.

Well, the evening news just informed me
that tomorrow will be more of the same.
What a shame. In the morning I had planned,
right after breakfast and my second or third cup
I was going to dig deep, and whip a happy poem up.
"Oh! Well, maybe tomorrow."

The Due Date

The Shakers said it would be over in
1792 but that prediction didn't hold true.
Jehovah's Witnesses stretched their
"due date" a bit long, not like the
Shakers before, and predicted between
1914 and 1994.

Other religious groups have also predicted
as well, when many will end up in Heaven
or in Hell. Just when I was beginning to feel
good, and my stress level down, and things
were finally going well, I'm now told the new
"Due date" will be here in just a spell.

This new *"due date"* is taken from an ancient
Mayan calendar which wise men of today do
tell, is December 21, 2012.

Since there is so little time, and I am feeling good,
my stress level is down, plus things are going swell.
If this date is assured, then I shall go peacefully, and
wish all mankind well.

The Good Old Days

When I was a young lad I spent all day laughing
and playing, precious time I seldom saved.

Years have passed and here I stand with a mop in my
hand, and a bucket full of suds, and floors I must scrub.

I don't understand, I was told SpongeBob was educational,
and I was darn good playing Pac' man.

The Letter

The badly marred body lying nearby, at a glance
could barely be identified. The leader knew
his name; it was easy to remember because it was
one of the same.

They had arrived the same day a year ago this very
May, so close to going home just one more day.
So many have died since this war began and here
I sit again with paper and pen.

How will I start this letter, what will I say? The words
are beginning to sound the same, and not able to find
new ones I feel ashamed. This one is even harder to
find the right words to say, because my twin lying out there
was killed on our birthday.

The Master's Bed

Where do I bark, where do I start, bad
news I fear. Drop your milk bones, pay
attention, and you there, stop scratching
your ear.

I know we get free medical, free food, free
room and board, plus grooming, but hard
times are coming I dread.

The Master is removing the ramps and stairs
next to the bed, which means, us old dogs won't
be able to climb aboard to rest our heads.

When I think of all the loving we have given
him over the years, losing my spot on his
bed is enough to bring me to tears.

If he makes me lay on a mattress or blanket
next to his bed I'm going to eat a whole box of
milk bones and play dead.

When he sees me lying there with my stomach
all swollen from eating those milk bones,
and my tongue hanging out, it will give him
such an awful fright.

I know it's not nice pretending to be dead, and
to give the Master such a fright, but can you
think of a better place to snuggle up during
those cold winter nights?

The Meeting

If we could bring together all the different
gods, what do you think they would say
if they were shown a video depicting the
condition of the world today?

You think they would bow their heads in
shame, or start pointing fingers to place the
blame, or quickly open and review their
books to see why their words are being
over looked?

Some say that there is only one god, while
others say; there are many, and have written
books to justify or explain their chosen god's
plan.

I do hope the gods and their believers can
come to an agreement, and straighten things
out, because I hear talk of burning in hell,
and it's giving me an awful fright.

The Money Chase

Major indexes falling, the Dow has hit a five-year low
the market is walloped, where did all the money go?

Redemption notices from clients who want their
money back, but so far its not as bad as the thirties;
window jumping, and heart attacks.

The market problems seem to have spread all over
the world. Investors disgusted and demoralized
and can no longer believe the Federal Reserve.

Not to worry though, relief is on the way. All the
Presidential candidates assured us during their
debates just the other day.

Now if we cannot believe them, who can we believe?
Hey! I am trying to be serious here, so stop the laughing
please.

The Nightmare

One minute she was standing there, the next
minute she was gone., Taken so quickly, as she
screamed and kicked to free herself from
unwanted arms.

She was just a child when abducted that
summer day, but after months of abuse
her life had changed, and so did her youth.

Sexually abused, injected with drugs, by the
scum of the earth, not worthy of being called
thugs.

Eventually rescued and returned to her loved
ones who did everything they could to help
her ease the pain, ensuring her, she wasn't
to blame.

Although she felt their love and knew it was not her
fault, she still couldn't shake the horrible nightmares
that controlled her every thought.

Body and mind so badly abused by earth's scum,
there all alone in the dark, she allowed death to come.

The Other Side

Isn't it nice to now have all the answers,
no longer needing to believe; no more
suffering, finally resting, finally free.

Everything became crystal clear the moment
I closed my eyes, but sadly all the loved ones
near thought they watched me die.

Little do they know, I am alive and well here
on the other side, but unable to return and tell.

I hope they will cultivate the seeds I left
in their hearts, sprinkling them daily with
the love and tenderness I taught.

I know if the seeds I placed in their hearts
are able to grow and blossom throughout
the year, I will no longer be thought of as dead
to them, but always alive and near.

The Sorry Farm

Stop wasting your time being apologetic
about past mistakes when you
meant no harm. Otherwise, you will spend
all your time on the . . . *"Sorry Farm."*

When you came into this life, you were helpless,
eyes closed, and full of fright even before you had
time to adjust to the light. Then a stranger slapped
you across your butt and sent you a flight.

From then on, you relied on others to teach you
more of the right, then that which was wrong, in
the hope of lessening your time at the . . .
"Sorry Farm."

It's wasn't an easy task, but they did the best they
could before saying good bye. So go forward with
the best that was given, and stop all the . . .
would-I, could-I or should I . . . at the Sorry Farm.

The Warlord's Children

Give him a gun, what the hell; he has
nothing to live for at the age of twelve.
Teach him to kill all that I choose. Should
he resist, deprive him of shelter and food.

He has no family. I killed them
during the last raid, so he should
be thankful that his life I saved.

I must continue to kill, rape, and take
all I can, for I am the New Warlord
of this god forsaken land.

Men have come here from far off shores
and took what I could never afford.
Now it's my turn to take all I can, and
children such as him will help me reach
this end.

Don't feel sad for the children under my
control, or bother to search your souls.
Celebrate your Christmas and New Year as
always, and let your good times continue
to roll.

Until Tomorrow

We were somewhat scattered in earlier days,
and in later years went different ways. However,
never too far, to hear each other's calls.

Our oldest sister Dorothy was the first to go. Now
another was chosen to be next, so again we have
come together, my sister and brothers, this time, to lay
our baby sister Judy to rest.

Who will be next? Whose name will be called?
I cannot help but wonder as I reflect on what has
happened to us all.

The questions life after death, light or darkness,
joy or sorrow, our departed sisters have the answers.
But we, my sister and brothers, must wait until tomorrow.

What's Up With That?

When I see someone wearing a cross
with or without the son of God there on
display, I say to yourself "what's up with that,"
is that a fashion statement or the "in thing" of the day?

I thought it had significance, and depicted
a certain way of life, not another piece of
jewelry to be worn with the rest of one's glitter
when they are out and about.

I do not wish to be judgmental, but strange thoughts
go through my mind, when I see the cross displayed
on various body parts from time to time.
"What's up with that?"

Why this way

I cannot begin to imagine the pain and heartfelt hurt
when they learned how their children died that day.
If you wanted to take them Lord, could you have
found a more humane way?

To use flames and fumes to kill these little
children is more than I can understand, was there
some sort of heavenly joke to bring them into
this world to later cause hurt and pain?

What will you say to them Lord, when they stand
before you asking why, showing you their charred
bodies, and upset at you because you made their
fathers and mothers cry.

Death I know will eventually come, and we all must
understand, but to take these children in such a way
is hard to comprehend. This northern Mexican town will
live forever with this memory and pain for a very long time,
some will even question, why did you choose this way, Lord,
to take mine.

Wings

Come if you may, night or day,
in the cold of winter or the warmth
of May. My work here is done.

I'm ready to fly with the angels
far beyond the sun. Any set of
wings will do; pop on, permanent,
new or used, none will be refused.

I'm told the heavens are really pretty up
there, and since I've done good, the
Heavenly Father said, He is more then
willing to share.

About the Author

Born and raised in Baltimore Maryland, a proud father of two and grandfather of two. Joe served with honor in the United States Air Force for twenty years. He now lives in Las Vegas, Nevada with his wife Veronica.

Made in the USA
San Bernardino, CA
22 July 2014